T0286312

A DINOSAUR'S DAY

Deinonychus
GOES HUNTING

DK

MARIE BOLLMANN
ELIZABETH GILBERT BEDIA

Crafty. Curious. Clever.
This is Deinonychus.
Her name means "terrible claw."

Join this small but mighty
predator's high-energy day.

Ready or not, here we go!

As sunlight bursts over the horizon, **Deinonychus** is feasting.
She finishes the last of her early breakfast with her hunting group.

Her day has begun.

She watches as the rest of world wakes around her, and her keen nose alerts her that others are on the move.

Calls and cries echo
across the hazy sky
and thick forest.

Tenontosaurus, **Cedarpelta**, and other plant-eaters are looking for food.

Deinonychus leaves her hunting group to investigate.

She spies them. **Crafty.**

SNIFF!
SNIFF!
SNIFF!

The other dinosaurs stop. Then they SCATTER!

Why? Because Deinonychus is a carnivore.
And they don't want to be her next meal!

Lucky for them, she's still full from breakfast. **Phew!**

Besides, something else is happening, and Deinonychus is on high alert.

Her eyes widen.

Lifting her nose to the sky, she smells it.
Is it **Acrocanthosaurus**?

No. It's an angry storm rolling in.

BOOM! BOOM! BOOM!

Deinonychus flees. She is quick, and
runs as fast as her body can take her,
but the heavy rain soaks her downy feathers.

Deinonychus finds shelter under a rocky ridge.

She wait and waits.
Will the rain ever end?

Yawwwwn

She has a full belly and nowhere to go, so it is the perfect time for a nap.

When Deinonychus wakes up, the afternoon
sun is warming her feathered skin.

But what's that? The smell of something tasty.
Curious.

Her nose twitches and her strong croc-like mouth begins to drool.

Zephyrosaurus.
Is there a better way to spend the afternoon than chasing Zephyrosaurus?

Deinonychus doesn't think so. Is she ready?

Stiff tail to balance?
Check!

They are off!

Deinonychus zigs.

Zephyrosaurus zigs.

Zephyrosaurus zags.

Deinonychus zags.

Deinonychus closes in and jumps toward Zephyrosaurus. But...

the ground below shakes and **RUMBLES!**

Zephyrosaurus escapes, but Deinonychus **STUMBLES!**

She **TUMBLES** down, down, down into a mud-caked ravine.

A fallen conifer tree shows the way.

She sinks her sharp claws into the soft tree trunk. **Clever.**

She climbs up and jumps out of the ravine, using her powerful legs and her tail for balance.

It has been a big day!

All the rumbling and tumbling has
Deinonychus's tummy **grumbling**.

As the sun sinks below the horizon, Deinonychus rejoins her hunting group. She is ready to...

CHOMP!

Who was Deinonychus?

Deinonychus was a carnivore, which meant it hunted other animals for food.

Deinonychus lived about 110 million years ago in what is now North America.

Deinonychus was covered in downy feathers.

Deinonychus had razor-sharp teeth and deadly claws.

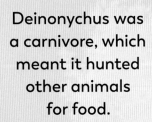

Deinonychus was about 10ft (3m) long, and weighed about as much as a large person.

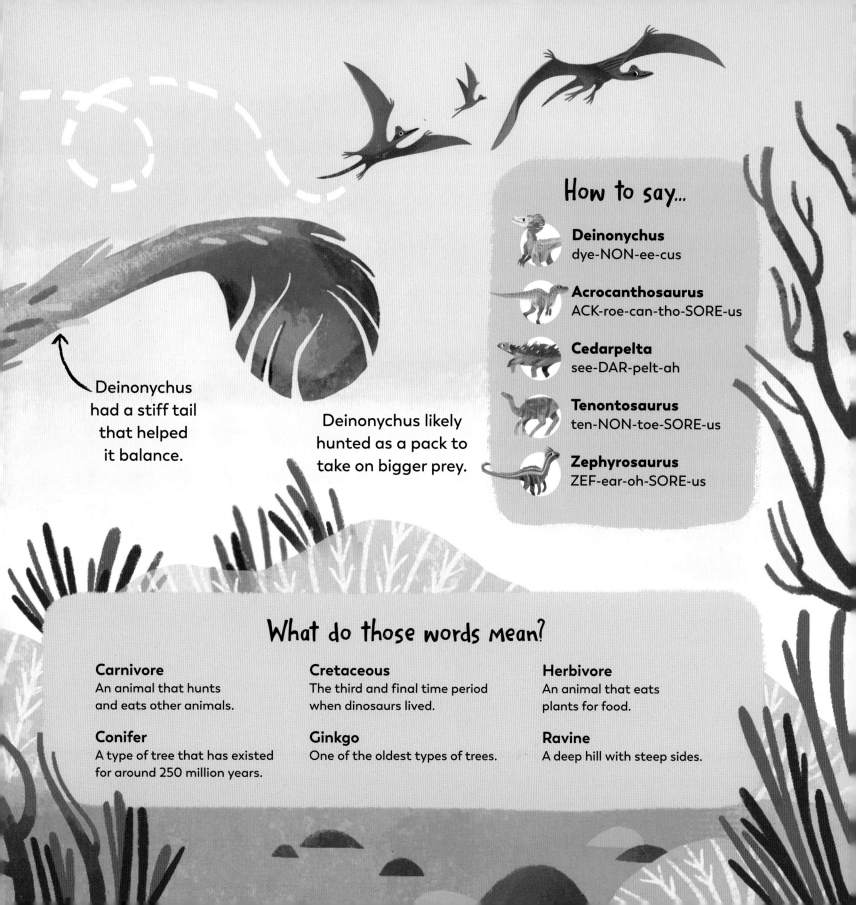

Deinonychus had a stiff tail that helped it balance.

Deinonychus likely hunted as a pack to take on bigger prey.

How to say...

Deinonychus
dye-NON-ee-cus

Acrocanthosaurus
ACK-roe-can-tho-SORE-us

Cedarpelta
see-DAR-pelt-ah

Tenontosaurus
ten-NON-toe-SORE-us

Zephyrosaurus
ZEF-ear-oh-SORE-us

What do those words mean?

Carnivore
An animal that hunts and eats other animals.

Conifer
A type of tree that has existed for around 250 million years.

Cretaceous
The third and final time period when dinosaurs lived.

Ginkgo
One of the oldest types of trees.

Herbivore
An animal that eats plants for food.

Ravine
A deep hill with steep sides.

About the illustrator

Marie Bollmann is an illustrator who specializes in children's books. Marie was born in Münster, Germany, and is now based in Hamburg. She likes creating colorful, detailed illustrations, and her favorite dinosaur is Triceratops.

About the author

Elizabeth Gilbert Bedia is a former teacher and audiologist. She loves creating stories about our amazing world. She is the author of *Bess the Barn Stands Strong*, and *Balloons for Papa*. She lives in central Iowa with her dinosaur-loving family. You can visit her at www.elizabethgilbertbedia.com.

About the consultant

Dougal Dixon is a Scottish paleontologist, geologist, author, and educator. He has written more than 100 books, including the seminal work of speculative biology *After Man*, and award-winning *Where the Whales Walked*.

Illustrator Marie Bollmann
Text for DK by Elizabeth Gilbert Bedia & Et Al Creative
Acquisitions Editors Fay Evans, James Mitchem
US Senior Editor Shannon Beatty
Project Art Editor Charlotte Bull
Consultant Dougal Dixon
Publishing Coordinator Issy Walsh
Production Editor Abi Maxwell
Production Controller Magda Bojko
Deputy Art Director Mabel Chan
Publishing Director Sarah Larter

First American Edition, 2023
Published in the United States by DK Publishing
1745 Broadway, 20th Floor, New York, NY 10019

Illustrations copyright © Marie Bollmann 2022
Copyright © 2023 Dorling Kindersley Limited
DK, a Division of Penguin Random House LLC
23 24 25 26 27 10 9 8 7 6 5 4 3 2 1
001–327019–Feb/2023

All rights reserved.
Without limiting the rights under the copyright reserved above, no part of this publication may be reproduced, stored in or introduced into a retrieval system, or transmitted, in any form, or by any means (electronic, mechanical, photocopying, recording, or otherwise), without the prior written permission of the copyright owner.
Published in Great Britain by Dorling Kindersley Limited

A catalog record for this book
is available from the Library of Congress.
ISBN 978-0-7440-6005-8

DK books are available at special discounts when purchased in bulk for sales promotions, premiums, fund-raising, or educational use. For details, contact:
DK Publishing Special Markets,
1745 Broadway, 20th Floor, New York, NY 10019
SpecialSales@dk.com

Printed and bound in China

For the curious
www.dk.com

This book was made with Forest Stewardship Council™ certified paper – one small step in DK's commitment to a sustainable future. For more information go to www.dk.com/our-green-pledge

FSC
www.fsc.org
MIX
Paper | Supporting responsible forestry
FSC™ C018179